To Nanci
8/3

1.

AFTERGLOW

AFTER-GLOW

The Excitement of Being Filled with the Spirit

Sherwood E. Wirt

Foreword by Kenneth Chafin

**ZONDERVAN
PUBLISHING HOUSE** OF THE ZONDERVAN CORPORATION
GRAND RAPIDS, MICHIGAN 49506

AFTERGLOW
© 1975 by The Zondervan Corporation
Assigned to Sherwood E. Wirt 1976

Third printing 1976

Library of Congress Cataloging in Publication Data

Wirt, Sherwood Eliot.
    Afterglow: the excitement of being filled with
the Spirit

        1. Wirt, Sherwood Eliot.   2. Revivals — Canada.
I.   Title.
BR1725.W56A32   269'.2'0924   [B]   75-21122

Scripture quotations, unless otherwise indicated, are from *The King James Version* or represent the author's paraphrase of that version. *The Revised Standard Version* is copyright © 1946, 1952 by the Division of Christian Education of the National Council of Churches of Christ in the United States of America. *The Living Bible* is copyright © 1971 by Tyndale House Publishers, Wheaton, Illinois.

Printed in the United States of America

To my brothers and sisters

in the Afterglow ministry

Contents

Foreword

Afterglow is one of the most helpful books I've read in years.

It is believable. The people and relationships, the tensions and frustrations are easy for real human beings living in today's world to identify with.

It is a book with integrity and authenticity mainly because it is written out of a personal experience that is dealt with honestly. Sherwood Wirt started to stand on the sidelines and observe a spiritual awakening in Canada. That moving of God's Spirit changed him and began to reflect itself in every relationship of life and in all the experiences that are common to man. As a friend of many years I have observed the change in him.

It is a probing book. It is almost impossible to read the book without asking questions about yourself, your happiness, your goals, and your relationships. Yet as you ask the questions, you realize they have been in the back of your mind all along.

It is a wholesome book. As the struggle for a life of meaning and direction is articulated, the great resources in God's presence are celebrated. The answers found and applied to life are as believable as the problems presented.

It is superb writing. The book would be good if it were the first effort of an aspiring author because of the experience it chronicles. But because this took place in the life of one of the most disciplined writers in the church, we are doubly blessed. The chapters are short. The dialogue brisk. The flow natural.

Afterglow is Sherwood Wirt's best work. It is far too good a book to limit to pastors and staff. I want to recommend it to everyone who truly seeks a Spirit-filled life.

DR. KENNETH CHAFIN

South Main Baptist Church
Houston, Texas

Preface

It has been my unusual privilege for fifteen years to follow Billy Graham in a journalistic capacity while he has evangelized on six continents in the name of Jesus Christ.

In recent months I have taken odd moments to record God's unexpected working on a much smaller scale — the scene of my own inner life. This working has affected my temperament, my outlook, and even certain assignments on the Graham team. Who would have imagined a few years ago that I would be speaking to thousands of pastors and laymen in North and South America and Asia on the Spirit-filled life? What I have been telling them is the content of these pages.

The Afterglows described — occasions of sharing and prayer that follow a preaching service — are still being held as the Spirit leads. In that sense the Canadian revival is still with us. We have discovered that the open need in our churches is past all imagining.

Some of these chapters were composed in high-flying aircraft; other chapters in London, Barcelona, Toronto, and Rio de Janeiro; still others in various parts of the United States. I am grateful to the teachers whose influences have shaped my life (including "Mother"); and this work is in part an expression of thanksgiving and praise to God for them.

To Kersten Beckstrom, assistant editor of *Decision* magazine, go my warmest thanks for preparing and editing the typescript of yet another book. And to my co-laborers on the staff of *Decision*, my friends in the Minnesota Christian Writers' Guild, and my wife, Winola, go orchids of appreciation for valuable and constructive suggestions.

Minneapolis, Minnesota　　　　　　　　　　S.E.W.
April 1975

Preface to the Second Printing

The occasion of a second printing of this little volume gives me opportunity to say "Thank you" once again to God for the filling of his Spirit. The reception this little book has had — far exceeding anything I have previously written — makes me conscious anew of the deep need of our churches, and the ability of Jesus Christ to meet that need. May your "afterglow" long endure!

S.E.W.

Minneapolis, Minnesota
March 1976

AFTERGLOW

1

The Disappearance

I couldn't figure it out. There I was, sitting in the same easy chair, in the same room, with the same wife, and the same job, and I was happy. I felt a silly grin cracking my face. A doggerel tune danced through my head: "We'll give the glory to Jesus . . . "

The television set was on, but it showed little to smile about. Minnesota's weather was south of zero. Cambodia had been invaded. The stock market was slumping like a wet dandelion. And there I sat with that Cheshire grin, not able to understand why.

My wife lay on the davenport reading the newspaper and munching pretzels. ("My medication requires salt" was her explanation.)

"Honey," I said, struggling to express my mood. "You're a fine woman. Do you know that?"

She muttered something incomprehensible.

"I mean it," I said. "Furthermore, I believe that you've treated me better than I've treated you."

Afterglow

"That's true," she said, turning the page.

"Would you like to play a game of Scrabble?"

"No, thanks."

I know what it is, I thought. I've been filled with the Spirit. That meeting on Sunday night . . .

"Anything I can do for you, dear?" I went on recklessly.

"You can carry down those three boxes to the basement that I asked you to carry ten days ago."

I got to my feet with the air of a man who has just decided to kick a bad habit.

The fact was that nothing had taken a turn for the better. It was all muddling along as usual. What I had hoped for had failed to materialize. All the sources of irritation in my life were still there. I had not been to an emotional religious meeting, nor was I taking a trip.

But I had a contentment that was not there yesterday. The bitter taste of life was gone.

For years I had cocked my ear to a little voice that whispered, "If only . . . if only . . . ." Where was that voice?

For years I had plugged along trying to serve the Lord and adjusting to disappointments. Now I was savoring the realization that there is no disappointment in Jesus.

For years I had carried in my viscera a burning resentment toward certain people. It had disappeared!

I came up from the basement thinking about the loyal, faithful, devoted, loving partner God had given me. As I passed the refrigerator I asked, "Would you like some ice cream?"

Winola rattled the papers. "That won't get you out of the doghouse."

"Ice cream?" I repeated.

"I guess so," she said.

2

The Missing Piece

On the previous Sunday night, January 9, 1972, about twenty-five people from different churches had gathered in the basement of a church in Minneapolis.

They had just been dismissed from a service upstairs. The speakers were two Canadians, Harry and Evelyn Thiessen, and they had told how God had caused them, after twenty years of an increasingly bleak marriage, to fall in love with each other all over again.

It happened, they said, during the revival in Winnipeg a month earlier. But the revival wasn't a big outburst of excitement; rather it was a quiet working of the Holy Spirit in the lives of frustrated believers.

Anybody can be revived, they insisted, if he will deal honestly with his problem, pray for the crucifixion of self, and then ask for the filling of the Holy Spirit. They quoted Luke 11:13: "If you therefore, being evil, know how to give good gifts to your children, how much more will

Afterglow

the Father in heaven give the Holy Spirit to those who ask him?"

Fair enough; and besides, it was eight-thirty and time to go home. So most of the sensible people went.

And now here we were, the ones who were left, sitting in a circle and looking at one another.

A chair had been placed in the center, and Harry was speaking. "This is an Afterglow," he said. "We are here to pray. If someone would like prayer, we will pray with him. We can kneel here by this chair or go somewhere else." No one stirred.

I began to fidget. I was the one who, after listening to their testimony in Winnipeg three and a half weeks earlier, had invited Harry and Evelyn to come across the border and talk about the revival. In fact, I had paid their air fare from Manitoba. Earlier that evening they had told how the Afterglows had been used in churches all over western Canada with great spiritual results.

So here we were in an Afterglow. And it had bombed. Now what?

Looking around, I noticed that people were beginning to act embarrassed. Perhaps I could lift the tension by asking prayer for myself. Not that I needed it particularly, although one could always use . . .

I began to speak, and (to borrow a phrase of Augustine's) God cut the strings of my tongue. What was hidden in me spilled out: bitterness, hurt, longing, the sense that life had ganged up on me, resentment toward others.

Yes, I had things going for me, but they weren't going anywhere. In personal satisfaction the equation wasn't working out. I was helping Billy Graham, but no one was helping me. Something was lacking — something in me, no doubt. But a piece was missing, and it seemed to be the most important piece.

And I hadn't the muggiest idea as to what it was or

what to do about it.

Soon hands were being laid on my shoulders, my head. People were kneeling alongside me and praying for me. Then my turn came to pray, and I did so — fervently, eloquently, and, I thought, adequately. I asked God to help me be this and do that.

I finished and tried to get up, but hands held me down. Then I heard Harry's voice: "Ask God to crucify you."

Crucify me? I wasn't even sure the idea was theologically sound. "To do what?" I stammered.

"Nail you to the cross" was the reply.

Well, he had me, this bearded civil engineer from Manitoba. What could I do? I did as directed.

"Now ask God to fill you with his Spirit and thank him for it."

I swallowed and obeyed. Someone started a chorus, and they let me go. I went back to my seat considerably subdued, feeling awkward and foolish.

Evelyn smiled in my direction. "You probably don't have much of a sensation of blessing now," she said. "Don't worry. The feeling will come later — and how!"

She was right. It came. And it has never left.

3

The Divine Solution

"The Holy Spirit used a divine solvent," said Evelyn, "to dissolve the bitterness in my heart."

I had to think about that.

It had worked after twenty years for them. What about us? Our marriage had thirty years of mileage. You might say we had made a rather good adjustment of it. But start tampering with something that has been on the road that long, and the whole thing might fall apart. To overhaul a worn engine might be a good idea, but to overhaul a marriage? That was something else.

Nevertheless those words spoken in my hearing left their mark on me. If only the memories would disappear! Every day of my life some hoary memory would float back from the graveyard of the past, bringing to mind an unpleasant event that had occurred along the route.

In desperation I went over the clichés of the good life which I had heard and had passed on to others.

"Be a good forgiver." The trouble was, I couldn't

17

forget. I took considerable pleasure in remembering how badly I had been abused. Instead of singing the sweet song of salvation, I reveled in thoughts of my mistreatment.

"It's water under the bridge now." So it was; but the devil was building new bridges downstream.

"Let it lie." But if it wouldn't lie? If it insisted on rearing its head?

"Patch things up." I tried; the patches came off.

"Bury the hatchet." I did; but knowing the spot where it was buried, I would insist on digging it up.

"Drop it into the sea of forgetfulness." Such words bear the stamp of pulpit language. I never did locate a map with that sea on it.

"Accept the situation." I knew about the pastoral counseling approach; unfortunately this physician could not heal himself. It seemed to me that I not only accepted the situation, but soaked and wallowed in it and could never get away from it.

And now it was proposed that I give it up; that all those hurt feelings would then dissolve in a solution of love, and the hatchet would self-destruct.

It had been years since I applied the Gospel to my own, personal, inner life. I turned to the Bible for help. In Paul's Letter to the Ephesians I found the verse "Let all bitterness, and indignation, and wrath ... be removed from you."

Someone else would have to do that; it was beyond me.

In Isaiah 61 I read, "The Spirit of the Lord God is upon me ... to give unto them beauty for ashes, the oil of joy for mourning, the garment of praise for the spirit of heaviness."

Was that then this solvent — the oil of joy given by the Holy Spirit? Joy was what I seemed to have in short supply. Oh, I had joy in the Lord. I loved to think about Christ. But joy in other compartments of my life? No.

Instead, a spirit of heaviness. A drag.

It seemed to me that I was standing alongside a giant conduit in the middle of the desert. Inside I could hear the water running as it was conveyed to some distant point; but it did nothing to slake my thirst, and I knew no way to reach it.

So I waited on the Lord and he inclined his ear to me. He heard my complaint — not about others this time, but about myself.

Of course words are easy to give out, and God knows that too. But when I informed him that I was abdicating the throne of my life (my Christian life, that is); when I said that my ego had been deposed and driven into exile; when I asked him to crucify me, he accepted my statement and fulfilled my request.

In his own time and at his own pleasure he sent a divine solvent into this troubled heart. It was like the warmth of the sun burning off the layers of fog.

I don't know just how the love came in, but I know that all the bitterness I held against others — including those near to me — disappeared.

Resentment — hostility — hurt feelings — you name it.

They all dissolved. Evaporated.

Went.

4

The Other Person

"You can't change anybody, but God can change you."

When I first heard this from our revived Canadian friends, I passed it off as another evangelical bromide. Since then it has revolutionized my whole attitude toward people.

I was a reformer at heart. One of my basic aims in life was to straighten out the other person. My Christianity was a means to that end.

Winola, of course, was at the top of the list. Mind you, no one appreciated my wife more than I did. I recognized her virtuosity, her attractiveness, her generous nature, her high standards, her brilliant mind; I loved her sense of humor and was genuinely proud of her achievements. I considered her altogether a remarkable person.

But she needed to shape up.

"Honey," I would say to her in my unhoneyed way, while watching her plow through one purse after another, "I bought you a steel file. If you would just keep your papers in it, you wouldn't lose them all the time."

It's odd how a simple, helpful comment like that will irritate a wife. I was merely trying to get Winola to change her ways for her own good.

"Look," she would come back at me, "I know exactly where I leave things. My only problem is you. You come along and throw out half my stuff. No wonder I can't find anything."

Once the conversation has been wrenched out of context by such deliberately *ad hominem* remarks, it can only deteriorate. My efforts to improve my wife's habits were a lamentable failure.

Attempts to give advice to other people met with similar responses. My experience in various fields seemed to qualify me to help a lot of people; it was amazing how few seemed to take advantage of it.

As a Christian, for example, I was aware that many of my church acquaintances were simply not living according to the principles of the Bible. I knew what they needed. Their attitudes, their values, were wrong. If they would listen to me — but they wouldn't.

"You can't change anybody, but God can change you." Well, he did change me. I don't fully understand how it happened, but now, instead of handing out unsought advice, I tell people what I appreciate about them. They seem to enjoy hearing it.

If they want the facts, I give them the facts. But I do not attempt to change people. I leave it to the Holy Spirit to work according to his own pleasure.

If Winola loses something, I don't entertain her with a free lecture and advise her to adopt a different life-style. I just help her to find it. She has left me some beautiful openings, but I haven't walked into them. And strange to report, she is doing the same by me.

In short, we have a brand-new love affair going.

Now that I have ceased trying to give advice, occasionally people come asking for it. What a temptation! But I have to tell them I have traded my couch for a carpet. I'll get down on my knees and pray with anyone. I'll look at Scripture with anyone.

The rest, as Shakespeare said, is silence. Or it might better be. God is the source of wisdom; I direct people to him.

5

The Index Digit

Love, I felt, was my outstanding personality trait. I came across as a really lovable guy — to myself.

Some didn't get the message, but I excused them, reasoning that many people today are wrestling with psychological problems. Others, I suspected, were locked into their sins.

And of course it was hard even for a "dedicated" Christian like me to love some people.

I belonged to the "however" school of Christianity, which is more popular than is realized. It differs only in degree from the carnal school of behavior which functions under the code "Do others as they do you, but do them first."

My adaptation went along these lines: "I believe in the New Testament; however . . . "

"I am a disciple of Jesus Christ; however . . . "

"I treat people with Christian love; however . . . "

In other words, such Christianity as I displayed

25

depended about 95 percent on the kind that was displayed toward me.

As might be expected, this approach did not carry very far. On one occasion some years ago I was hoping to be called to pastor a new church being organized in a highly promising location. It was a half-million-dollar enterprise.

The man to whom I applied informed me, "We are looking for a person of national importance to lead that congregation. It's going to become one of our great churches. But I'll be glad to add your name to the list." I was serving a congregation of seventy active members.

During a conversation at lunch that day a friend remarked to me, "If a guy doesn't make it by the time he is forty-five, he'll never make it."

I came home discouraged. I was almost forty-four.

Putting on my old clothes, I went out into the yard to trim the hedge. Winola joined me, and the conversation soon became warm and sticky. After a pause she said, "They won't ask us to that church."

"Why not?"

"Because," she said snipping a branch of wisteria, "we're so mean to each other."

Her prediction came true.

The unconscious aim of my ministry in those days was to make a showing. I wanted to prove what I could do so that I would be given something more important to do.

Some church sociologists made a survey of our city and devised an "evangelistic index" — the number of new members per year in ratio to total membership. That index was what interested me: A reputation for taking in members meant a call to a bigger church.

It never occurred to me that the one thing God wanted from me was to show love to people — starting with Winola.

I could see a lot of things lacking in my wife. But I couldn't see the biggest lack of all — the lack of my love. To be sure, I loved her, but there is a love that cherishes, and it was somehow missing from my makeup. This myopic condition went on for years, both during my pastorates and after I became an editor.

One day late in 1971 I read that strange report from Canada. Curious things were taking place in some congregations in the western provinces. Brothers and sisters, it was said, had been reconciled to each other; shoplifted articles had been returned; crimes were being reported by the culprits; church feuds were being resolved; pastors were confessing their pride.

But then I heard this word: "We're walking knee-deep in love up here."

I was looking for external evidence of revival that would stack up alongside the great revivals of the past. Guns laid on the pulpit, perhaps, or drugs flushed down the toilet.

But love? Knee-deep? I wasn't sure how to handle that.

It had no index digit.

6

"I Believe in Hell"

In the middle of January 1972 I sat at the typewriter in my office thinking about my wife. I picked up the telephone and dialed home.

"Hello, sweetheart," I said.

"What's wrong?" asked the voice at the other end.

"Nothing. I just wanted to know how you're getting along."

"Isn't this rather unusual? You left instructions that you didn't wish to be disturbed at the office."

"Oh, well," I said, "I've been filled with the Holy Spirit."

"I'll make a note of it," said Winola.

"I love you," I went on.

"I'm thinking about it," she said. "I'll give it about three weeks." She had been through my reformation programs before.

"Not it," I corrected her. "Him."

"Listen," said Winola. "I knew the Holy Spirit

29

when you were in left field someplace. Don't you try to
teach me."

Winola was right; she had become a child of God
long before she met me. Our first encounter took place on a
June day in the year 1940, on the top sun deck of the S.S.
Alaska, on a cruise from Seattle to Juneau and Skagway.

Winola was a blithe spirit from Pennsylvania who
had a way of making friends easily. I knew little about her,
but it didn't take me long to fall in love with her.

At the time, I was planning to enter a theological
seminary without really knowing why. Theology was
farthest from my thoughts as we talked on the sun deck.
But there came a time when we leaned against the fantail
on the afterdeck, studying the wake as the ship threaded its
way through the Inside Passage; and the conversation
turned to religion.

Winola seemed to feel something was lacking in
my grasp of the subject. In her bewilderment she asked,
"Aren't you saved?"

She had me. I'd heard the words before, but they
didn't fit into my environment. Saved from what? I had
picked up no firm word on heaven during my years at the
university, and it didn't trouble me. I reasoned that if such
a place as heaven existed, it meant I was going there.

"Tell you what," I said, slipping my arm about
her. "We'll talk about these things after I get into seminary
and we'll grow together. How's that?"

"Not me," she said, moving away slightly. "I'm
staying where I am."

"What do you mean?" I asked, alarmed. "Don't
you want to grow? Doesn't everybody?"

"I'm an evangelical," she stated. "I believe in
hell. And I believe in the second coming of Jesus Christ."

I almost fell over the gunwale. Winola seemed so
normal to me, so pretty, so sensible. "Science doesn't teach
that," I said.

"I don't care," she retorted. "My mother teaches it, and that's good enough for me."

"Your mother — ?"

"Yes. She's taught a Bible class for years."

"Where did she — ah — I mean, did she study somewhere?"

"Naturally. We go to the Montrose Bible Conference every summer. It's right near our home."

"Oh."

"All the great Bible teachers go there. Don't you believe the Bible?"

"Well," I gulped. "I'm not sure. I've started reading Goodspeed's translation."

"Well, I believe it. Dr. Torrey used to say at Montrose, 'God said it, Christ did it, I believe it, that settles it.'"

"Settles what?"

"Whether you're saved, silly."

Since we were already informally engaged, I decided to change the subject. We were in love, and her mother was six thousand miles away.

Winola did not know the Scriptures as her mother did, or she would have been more wary of me. But be that as it may, she became my wife, for better and for worse.

7

Family Devotions

In 1941, a year after our shipboard romance had led to its happy result, a petite Pennsylvania widow sold the ladies' shop she had kept for thirty years and moved to the Pacific Coast.

This was "Mother," Faith McCain Wells, artist, musician, and student of Scripture. She had become my mother-in-law, and her arrival in Berkeley, California, set the stage for the Great Theological Confrontation.

I was a student at a seminary with liberal views consistent with my own upbringing, and I was blissfully unaware of what was coming. My professors were brilliant scholars and earnest social idealists. I had no trouble identifying generally with their humanitarian outlook.

Having grown up knowing nothing whatever about the Bible, I listened to what they had to say about it, though their critical approach left me with little incentive to preach. They claimed that the Bible is a valuable historical document which, like all human creations, is marred by discrepancies and inconsistencies. They even declared that the revered authors of the "sacred" books were not above faking it when it suited their purpose.

For a textbook we students used *An American Translation of the Bible,* by Edgar J. Goodspeed and others, since it was deemed the best English rendition available at the time. We were told to mark various strands in the Old Testament with different-colored crayons. It seems a German scholar named Eissfeldt considered these strands the original materials which some unknown redactor had patched together to make the Bible.

The Great Confrontation took place in Mother's parlor where, each evening after dinner, she produced a thick, black Scofield Bible filled with alarming notes and handwritten scrawls. (The scrawls, I learned, were notes of sermons delivered by eminent divines who were totally unknown in the halls of my seminary.)

Our evening devotions consisted of one chapter, read aloud in turns, followed by a Gospel song I had never heard before, and prayer.

Winola had her own Scofield Bible. That made it two Scofields against one Goodspeed.

We went round and round, each reading two verses, until suddenly I went mute. Mother and daughter waited patiently, but I had nothing to say. Finally they picked it up, and the reading was lamely concluded.

What had happened was simple: I had been left up Salt Creek by Professor Goodspeed.

This scholar had translated the New Testament in his own highly selective way. When he thought a particular passage lacked sufficient support from the earlier manuscripts, he simply dropped it. The traditional numbering system of the King James Version, of course, doesn't allow for dropped verses. So when Mr. Goodspeed jumped the text from Luke 24:11 to 24:13 (to cite one example), he left me without any verse to read. He gave no explanation, provided no footnote; and there I sat.

I was ashamed to say what had happened because my Goodspeed Bible was already suspect.

The end of the chapter reading was just the beginning of devotions. Mother would remark, "Wasn't that a good chapter? Let's read the next one." Or more frequently she would remark, "Mr. Scofield has a good note here. I'll just share it."

"But, Mother — ," I would protest. (Tomorrow's quiz on the Graf-Wellhausen theory of Pentateuchal chicanery seemed vastly more important than the opinions of some preacher from Texas.)

"You need sound teaching, Sherwood," Mother said gently, looking over her bifocals.

"I'm getting excellent teaching, Mother. My professors are world-famous men. They've excavated – "

"They're not straight on doctrine," said Mother. "It says in the Scripture they have a zeal, but not according to knowledge."

"Who has a zeal?"

Mother rocked in her chair. "Let God be true and every man a liar."

Now the issue was joined. We were eyeball to eyeball, and I blinked.

The "note" in the Scofield Bible proved to be nearly a page in length. It spoke clearly and firmly of hell, of apostasy, of the rapture, of tribulations and dispensations.

Then a tune was hoisted and we were into prayer. I was aghast. There was no way out of the trap.

So I became a Christian.

8

The Man Needs Help

Thirty years have passed since the Great Confrontation. It is now 1971 and "Mother" has been in heaven for ten years. And how is her reluctant convert doing?

In some ways Mother would be proud of him, no doubt. And how is he doing inside, where he lives? How is he getting along with her daughter?

Not so good. He needs help.

Over the decades he has accumulated considerable information of a religious nature. He prays; he reads his Bible, though of late he has been doing it the way he brushes his teeth — with his mind on something else.

He is loyal to Jesus Christ, but he is unhappy. And he is having trouble with his daydreams.

* * *

My condition was, in fact, like that of millions of other Christians. I had read books about the "deeper life," had sung songs about the "power in the blood," and had sat under Bible teachers of my own. As sincerely and responsibly as I knew how, I had committed my life to the Lord Jesus Christ.

With respect to the Holy Spirit, I knew who he was. I had a kind of theological appreciation of his person, work, gifts, and fruit. I was aware of the controversies that have swirled about the Holy Spirit since the early centuries of Christianity.

If only people didn't keep talking about him! It got so I associated him with sectarian movements and odd people (as I thought) who spoke in tongues and claimed esoteric experiences.

The subject was embarrassing. I tried to avoid it. When someone brought up the Holy Spirit at a midweek Bible study, I felt threatened and moved to the next verse.

For years the churches have been debating whether new believers become baptized in and filled with the Spirit at conversion, or whether some kind of "second blessing" takes place. Scripture is quoted freely to support differing viewpoints.

Not being Solomon, I can't settle the matter. The Holy Spirit is a mysterious Person. Yet we all know people, presumably Christians, who seem anything but Spirit-filled. Whether or not their theology is correct, they just don't love! To all intents and purposes the Holy Spirit remains for them locked in the sixteenth chapter of John.

That judgment is based not on what I know of others, but what I know of myself. It should be evident that the Holy Spirit had never filled me: I had never allowed him to take full possession of my self-life in the name of Jesus; or to pray through me and make me a vessel of his love.

I was like a vacuum cleaner. You take it out of the closet, fit the cord into the wall socket, switch on the motor, and the wheels turn, the machine moves, but nothing much happens. The dirt stays where it is on the floor.

Something is stuck in the hose.

I was like an Army prisoner being marched from the guardhouse to the mess hall. I looked free, walked free, used the vocabulary of freedom, but behind me was a bayonet.

When a Christian is not Spirit-filled, he has to go with the law. The law tells people what to do with their lives. And the law has a bayonet.

Had the Lord called me to himself during those years, I would have been home free. I knew I was saved for eternity, even though I did not know exactly when it happened.

(That is the case with more Christians than is generally recognized. We keep walking into deeper water until we are over our heads. We realize that faith is the basis of the Christian life. We are conscious of our salvation, and we know it to be the regenerating work of the Holy Spirit, but we have no idea at what moment we passed from death to life.)

As I read Scripture, at my conversion (whenever that was) all the resources of God's power had been made available to me by His Spirit. I just wasn't drawing on them!

So I was spiritually ready to meet my God; but I wasn't ready to live as a free soul. I was fit for death, but not for life.

And do I know when I was *filled* with the Holy Spirit? I certainly do. It took place when I asked the Lord to take me out of the way, to nail me to the cross, and to fill me with his love.

"I have been crucified with Christ, and it is no longer I who live, but Christ who lives in me" (Galatians 2:20, LB).

9

A Quiet Ministry

Late in January 1972 (shortly after the experiences described earlier), I was invited to fill a pulpit in Duluth, Minnesota, on a Sunday night.

No one in Duluth knew what had been going on in Canada. I myself wasn't sure what had happened. But of one thing I was sure: I didn't feel like driving 320 miles through Minnesota snow to preach one of the stale sermons I had used so many times.

I had been filled with the Spirit! And so had some others. I telephoned three Minneapolis men whose lives had also been touched the night Harry and Evelyn had visited. Would they go to Duluth with me? They would.

That Sunday I hardly got a chance to preach. The men were so filled with what the Lord was doing in their lives, they couldn't stop talking, and I refused to interrupt. "Quench not the Spirit."

At the request of the congregation we went downstairs afterward for an Afterglow. We explained the

41

ground rules, and the people took over. They couldn't seem to get to the chair fast enough.

At a quarter to eleven it occurred to me that Monday was a workday, and we had a long way to go.

"Will you come back?" they asked us.

"Sure we will," we said, "but don't wait for us. You get together and pray for each other anytime you want."

The trip to Duluth opened a quiet ministry that has been going on ever since. I say "quiet," because God knows I am a braggart by nature and am always willing to take credit for what the Holy Spirit is doing. (Why forked lightning never strikes certain people is one of life's imponderables.)

Nevertheless the word got around despite my attempts to avoid the role of evangelical promoter. When a church inquired about the possibility of a team visit, a group of us from different churches took it as from the Lord. If the call was from out of town, we made up a caravan. If it was from nearby, a few revived people would drop in after their own church's Sunday evening service had finished.

"Have a cup of coffee ready after the service," we told the minister. "Expect some guests. Put a small rug in the center of your social hall, and arrange the chairs in a circle. You might have a box of facial tissue handy."

And no matter what the denominational persuasion of the congregation, the people who stayed for the Afterglow all looked beautiful as they came to the Lord for help.

They wanted more love in their lives, and they didn't know where to look for it or how to get it. We couldn't help them, but we knew who could. And we still do. There are no low inventories in God's warehouse.

* * *

Winola didn't make the trips with us. She stayed home with her problems, of which not a few had been caused by me.

10

Hitting the Chair

"You're great in the pulpit, but you're something else to live with." That was the kind of grade I received at home. Ministers having domestic problems learn to shrug off such talk, feeling it is unfair, unscriptural, and untrue.

However, by March of 1972 our home atmosphere was showing signs of improving. One night as I was helping her with the dishes, Winola asked me, "What do they do at those Afterglows?"

"Oh, nothing. Just pray."

"Why do they stay up so late?"

"We stay as long as there are people wanting prayer."

"Well," she said, "I might come to the next one."

In the course of time an Afterglow was requested by a suburban community church in Minneapolis on a Sunday evening. It began conventionally enough with coffee, a few choruses, and some introductions.

The visitor I introduced was Winola. She took a

45

Afterglow

seat beside me in the church basement circle.

As usual, the churchfolk were not sure what it was all about but were willing to watch. Since all we did was pray, a noticeable thawing took place as the evening progressed.

An elderly evangelist asked for prayer; then a tearful teen-aged girl, then a businessman who sounded troubled, then the minister.

One young man told us he was vice-president of a clothing chain, but felt his job was a cop-out. He had promised the Lord to serve him as a missionary; instead, like Jonah, he had taken a ship to Tarshish. So he prayed, and his wife prayed, and within three months they were on an Alaska Airlines jet, bound for a Christian radio station near Fairbanks. They are there today.

But Winola was struggling. She sat watching and listening and occasionally whispering. "Why do they make the seats so hard?" she asked at one point.

Moments became hours. The sounds were quiet but significant: a low voice speaking, the quiet murmur of prayer, an occasional sniffle, then a burst of song. I heard her whispering again: "Why do they always pray so long?"

"Really, that's all we're here to do — to pray," I whispered back.

"But they take so long!"

And they did. The Afterglow follows no time schedule. As long as there was anyone to pray, we prayed. The individual prayers were not long, but so many people asked for help!

When I looked at my watch at 11:15, there were still many who had not had an opportunity to ask for prayer. But Winola had had enough.

"I've held certain resentments for years," she announced to the circle, "and they've caused me nothing but grief. If this is what it takes to get rid of them, there's no sense waiting. I'm going to hit the chair."

46

Down she went on her knees, arms resting on the chair, and immediately a dozen others knelt down beside the chair and laid their hands on her.

What a battle took place in the heavenlies that night! A milestone was passed; Winola would never be the same. Some crooked ways were straightened and some rough places became plain.

After a person has spent a few hours kneeling with people he never saw before, he gains a fresh perspective. He sees that a community is not composed of twenty or fifty or five hundred churches; it consists of one church. And all the church people are being attacked by the same devil and are hurting in the same places and are uptight about the same sins: pride, lust, hostility.

And when they come to the cross and start to love, they are all filled with the same Spirit, whether they are eight years old or eighty.

The Afterglow finished at midnight. The twenty-five people who remained to the end stood in a circle, held hands, and sang a hymn. Then they drove out of the ghostly parking lot, leaving behind a half-used box of tissues, a few song sheets, and a building that was no longer the church.

Praise God, the church had become a living body.

11

The Invitation

Giving an invitation at the close of an evangelistic service was an agonizing experience for me.

I knew it was my duty, approved the idea, agreed with the theology behind it, recognized the need, and wanted to see souls come to the Lord. Furthermore, as a member of Billy Graham's team, I knew that many churches expected it of me.

But I dreaded it.

Of course, if one could be sure of a good response, one could make an appeal for commitments with confidence, not to say exuberance. But how can you predict a thing like that?

When I was invited to supply a pulpit, I would give the message everything I had. I would appeal to people in the pews to give their lives to Christ under any one of various categories (salvation, rededication, assurance, etc.). I would quote some of Billy Graham's favorite verses and announce the invitation hymn.

Afterglow

People stayed in their seats in droves.

After you have met that kind of response a few times, it gets to you. And you begin to get the message: "Better stick to your typewriter, boy, you don't have it."

Medhurst once said to Spurgeon, "I preach your sermons; why don't I get the same results you do from them?"

Spurgeon replied, "You don't expect conversions every time you preach, do you?"

"No, of course not."

"Well, that's why you don't have them."

Perhaps that was my problem — I didn't really expect much, and that's the way it worked out.

Helpful friends might point out that I don't exactly resemble Billy Graham. But neither did the apostle Paul, if early tradition is accurate. And neither did Spurgeon.

On December 15, 1971, I flew from Minneapolis to Winnipeg and sat under the preaching of the Reverend Wilbert L. McLeod, in whose Saskatoon church the Canadian revival had broken out two months earlier. As far as I was concerned it was a straight reporting job for the magazine I was editing; I anticipated no personal vibrations. Professional journalists don't wear their troubles on their sleeves.

I confess that what I saw amazed me. This man preached for only fifteen minutes, and he didn't even give an invitation! He announced the closing hymn, whereupon a hundred people came out of their seats and knelt at the front of the church. All he said was, "That's right, keep coming!"

Many were young. Many were in tears. All were from the Canadian Midwest, which is not known for its euphoria.

It could be said that what I was witnessing was revival. I believe it was. But what is revival?

50

Bill McLeod said, "Revival is God's finger pointed right at you." I didn't appreciate that. But the man knew his Scripture, and he spoke with authority.

And *he* didn't look like Billy Graham either.

12

The First Love

One Sunday in the summer of 1972 I was invited
to preach in a church in Minneapolis. I knew a division
existed among the people, so instead of delivering a sermon I conducted a Bible study.

Turning to the second chapter of the Book of
Revelation, I asked the congregation to examine with me
the first four verses. We used the King James Version, and
the people followed as I read the opening verse:

Unto the angel of the church of Ephesus write . . .

I explained that this was a letter dictated by Jesus
Christ to the apostle John. And since nobody knew exactly
who the "angel" might have been, I suggested that they
substitute the word "people," and then insert the name of
their church in place of "Ephesus." We went to the second
verse:

I know thy works and thy labor . . .

It was obvious, I said, that this was a hard-
working congregation. Every week scores of people con-

tributed man-hours and woman-hours to building up the life of the body. It was a generous, active church, and Jesus said, "I know about that." We continued:

And thy patience . . .

My visits to different parts of the world, I told them, had convinced me that the churches were filled with patient people. Many of the sermons they heard were disorganized and poorly illustrated. It was dull fare and unlikely to improve; yet they came back week after week. Were it not for patient Christians, the pews would long since have been emptied. And Jesus knew that.

And thou canst not bear with evildoers . . .

Jesus also knew, I said, that this was a church with high moral standards. It would not put up with wrongdoing in the midst. It was a church of character and principle.

And thou hast tried them which say they are apostles, and are not, and hast found them liars . . .

I pointed out that the church's orthodoxy was above reproach. It was a Bible-centered body of believers who would not tolerate false doctrine. Jesus honored his people for their faithfulness. On to the third verse:

And for my name's sake thou hast labored, and hast not fainted . . .

I asked them to note Jesus' acknowledgment that what was being done in the church was done for the sake of his name. And what was done in Jesus' name was done for Jesus. But now, I said, look at the fourth verse:

Nevertheless I have somewhat against thee, because thou hast left thy first love . . .

I asked what the "first love" was, adding that many people think it must be Jesus. But I asked how that could be, since in the preceding verse Jesus had just commended the church for doing great things for his name's sake?

And if the "first love" they had left was not Jesus, who was it?

I confessed I didn't know. I had looked in several commentaries and they were unclear. One writer said it was "the love they had at the first," which was hardly an explanation.

Since confusion existed regarding the meaning, I proposed to speculate. The "first love" they had left, I said, might have been their love for each other.

Why did I think so? Because Jesus was always talking about it. The New Testament is filled with it.

By this shall all men know that you are my disciples, if you have love one to another.

Owe no man anything but to love one another.

Beloved, if God so loved us, we ought also to love one another.

A new commandment I give unto you, that you love one another.

Book after book carries the same theme. I asked the people, "Do you catch the love in those verses? Because when you have caught it, you have it all."

Then I extended an invitation: "I'm not inviting you this morning to accept Jesus Christ as your personal Savior — though you may need to do it.

"I'm not inviting you to rededicate your life to Christ — though again, you may need to.

"I just wish to ask you a question: Do you want more love in your life? If you do, come down here in front during the singing of the hymn, and ask the Holy Spirit to fill you with love. He will do it."

And did they come? Did they come!

13

The Pointed Finger

One week later I was invited to preach in another church in the area. I also knew these people; in fact it was in their basement I had knelt and asked for the filling of the Holy Spirit.

From what I knew about this church and its challenges and difficulties, it seemed reasonable to assume its people could use an input of love. I asked them in turn to substitute the name of their church for Ephesus in Revelation 2, and we went from there. That morning the space in front of the pews was again filled with people seeking love.

Two weeks later I was asked to help out still another church that needed a supply in the minister's absence. In this case the congregation was almost totally unknown to me.

Now what? I prayed, "Lord, if there is something you want to say to these people, I trust you will just take over and say it."

By way of an answer, I was reminded of Bill

Afterglow

McLeod's word: "Revival is God's finger pointed right at you." What had been my problem? A lack of love.

On that sunny Sunday morning I told the pleasant, well-scrubbed congregation, "You love your minister, you love your country, you love the poor, you love the sinners, you love the folk in other churches, but you don't love each other."

When a preacher talks like that in public, he had better make sure he is Spirit-filled or he might find the deacons "waiting on him" afterward.

As it turned out, the Lord was right. These people had problems, and they wanted more love.

And so it has proved in churches in Mississippi, California, Wisconsin, North Carolina, Virginia, Iowa, Pennsylvania, South Dakota, Texas, Washington, Minnesota, and even Brazil. In many cases lay teams have come along with me to help in the prayer time and to share what the Holy Spirit has been doing in their lives. Their "testimonies" — if that's the word — are low key; they avoid what the theologians call "triumphalism." The Canadians have taught us to be plain and unvarnished.

Such a testimony might start with such a word as "I just got out of the hospital . . . " "We have a retarded child . . . " "The place where I work is a disaster area . . . " "My divorce papers came last week . . . "

What they tell people is that the Holy Spirit can fill the believer wherever and whenever he is prepared to ask for it.

They also urge the worshipers to remain for the Afterglow. They know what they are talking about! In a one-hour service God can do much, but in a three-hour Afterglow he can do more. These lay teams spend a large part of the hours that follow on their knees praying with and for people. They teach Christians how to pray for each other by doing it; and their ministry has become productive in a way none of them anticipated.

At the evening service a man sits half-listening. He has been enveloped in a sanctuary fog ever since he walked through the church door. As he listens to these honest people talking about the Holy Spirit, he begins to emerge from the fog. Is it possible they have something that can help him with his problem? Ten years in that church, and nobody has yet dug down to the root of it, mainly because he won't talk about it.

Sermons he can take or leave, but here is talk about human love, and he knows perfectly well love can help him out of his predicament. Is it possible — is it possible he could latch onto some of it?

He stays for the Afterglow, and when it comes his turn he asks for prayer. He kneels. His wife kneels beside him, puts her hand on him, and prays for him. His shoulders begin to tremble.

God is at work in his church.

14

Why They Pray

When people ask for prayer at an Afterglow, what is on their minds?

Anything!

One farmer had spent all Sunday afternoon trying to get his sow into the pen with her little pigs, but she wouldn't go. He became exasperated and lost his temper. That night he asked God to give him self-control.

Another man owned an auto body shop. The previous day he had sprayed the hood of a truck three times, and each time the paint had refused to stick. He also had a temper problem and asked for help.

One man had been to an earlier Afterglow in the same church and thought he would pass up this one. He drove home after the evening service, parked his car in the garage, shut the door, then opened it and drove back to the church. He told the people in the circle, "I really don't know what I'm doing here."

A lady he had never seen before, sitting by herself

in the back of the room, spoke up. "I do," she said.

As it turned out, the woman (who had introduced herself earlier as "nobody from nowhere") had a problem similar to the man's. Encouraged by his honesty, she offered her first prayer in three years.

A student with the highest marks in his high school knelt for prayer, saying he was weary of his perfectionism. "If I make a mistake," he said, "I want to make it for God."

A visitor from Hawaii told the group his family had just been wiped out in an automobile accident. He received compassion from God and sympathy from new Christian friends.

A model and television personality, currently appearing on talk shows coast to coast, asked for prayer that she might be patient and not run ahead of God.

A minister's wife said she was afraid she had a demon. Whenever she tried to read her Bible, the pages blurred. She asked for the perfect love that casts out fear.

An eleven-year-old girl waited until midnight for her turn to tell the others, "I have been a Christian all my life, but I have a very wicked heart."

A young woman asked for prayer because she was bothered by headaches. A bit later in the evening she spoke up again. "Headaches are not my real problem," she said. "I hate men. And I would like God to wash my soul clean."

We have found that Christians are wounded in the same places. When it comes to asking for prayer, there is no distinction of age, sex, status, denomination, or race.

I have prayed with people of every kind of background and skin color. Some grapple with feelings of pride, lust, or resentment. Others are hostile toward certain members of their church or toward their minister. Still others ask for more love for their wives or husbands. Because we encourage spouses to kneel and pray for their partners at the Afterglows, some moving scenes result.

One of the times I carry with me in memory is an Afterglow in a small-town church in the Midwest.

It had been a heartwarming evening, but a long one. An Indian pastor and his wife were present. A man who had mistreated his wife for years had asked for help. Now we had reached midnight, and five children were still waiting to be prayed for, all of them between ten and twelve years of age. (We invite parents of young children who wish prayer to speak up early, but these children had wanted to stay through.)

I suggested that we take the five youngsters together. We asked what they wanted prayer for. One said, "I want to pray that my daddy will be saved." Another, "I want to be a minister." Three of them said, "I want to be a better witness at school."

Together they knelt in the center of the circle, three boys and two girls. Around them knelt fifteen-to-twenty church people, some of them their parents. They prayed; then the children prayed.

The sound of those young voices lifted in prayer has never left me. They keep me from ever despairing of the church of Jesus Christ.

15

After the Glow

Beautiful things happen when people ask for prayer. Even more beautiful things happen after other people have bent their knees and prayed with them.

A young man who came to an Afterglow asked God to make him a better witness for Christ to strangers. The next day he stopped for breakfast at a restaurant. The man sitting beside him at the counter said to him, "You look as if you were out having a big time last night." It was an open door, and he walked through it.

A young probation officer brought his wife to the Afterglow at her parents' urging, even though he had been separated from her for some months and was living in his own apartment. Once it seems he had planned to become a minister, but at seminary a skeptical professor had disillusioned him.

The couple stayed about an hour at the prayer circle, then left. At a quarter to midnight, the Afterglow still in progress, he returned alone. The people there

Afterglow

stayed another hour, talking with him. He was a confused young man; but at last he bent to his Father's will and asked for prayer.

The family is back together and he has a different job.

Sometimes refreshments are served between the evening service and the Afterglow. I sat in a church social hall in Virginia drinking coffee and talking across the table to a young lady from the West Coast. When I learned what church she was from, I asked her, "Are you a Christian?"

"I'm not sure," she said. It was an answer I had anticipated, knowing her church.

At our urging, she stayed for the Afterglow. Two hours later she asked for prayer and received Jesus Christ as her Savior. Her new church undertook the responsibility for her Christian nurture.

One minister's wife stood to her feet after kneeling and being prayed for, and cried out, "I'm free at last!"

In another church a woman looked across the prayer circle at her pastor as she spoke. "For a long time I have had something against our minister," she said, "and he knows it. I felt I had to go outside my church to have an experience with God. When I came back here, the place seemed cold and heartless. Tonight I want to ask his forgiveness, and God's."

As she knelt, the minister joined in praying with her.

The next day, Sunday, she greeted him at the door after the service and there was a mutual expression of Christian love.

Ten days later he was dead, victim of a freeway traffic accident. When I telephoned the minister's home long-distance to comfort his wife and to pray with her, I remarked that the reconciliation with the lady church member had taken place in God's timing. Said the wife, "She's here now, staying with me."

A young American Indian who lived in a hotel came to the Afterglow being held in a nearby church. He asked for prayer and a few weeks later applied for and entered Bible school to prepare for Christian service. I don't know what motivated him, but I know *who* did.

A touring young Gospel musician dates his intimate relationship with Jesus Christ to an Afterglow that took place in a church where he had a singing engagement.

I listened one night in California to a fund-raiser for starving populations who had recently been under attack from the editors of a religious magazine. At the close of his address he said he was leaving early the next morning for New Orleans to oversee a food shipment to Honduras. The chairman said, "Let's pray for him." Several of us laid hands on him. Three weeks later I met him in Switzerland, and he told me how his heart had been warmed by the love of his Christian brothers and sisters that night.

I sat at lunch with a Congressman on the day before the voters were to go to the polls to reelect or reject him. A dozen of us had gathered simply for Christian fellowship. He, too, was under attack. As we prayed that God's will might be done in his life, hands were laid on him. It seemed to me that day that we came close to America's heart. The legislator went back to Washington with a love he didn't know he had.

Two free-lance writers joined a small group of us one summer in the mountains for what they later called "prayer on the rocks." As Christians they asked for prayer that they might receive a fresh touch from God. That fall they both found their markets.

The Afterglow is really misnamed; for many people it is a beginning. Often restitution has to follow, for as was shown at Saskatoon, restitution is a vital part of revival. People who ask for the filling of the Holy Spirit realize they now have to do things they have been putting off.

Afterglow

But here we have to be careful. Jesus did not speak simply of doing good, he spoke of "doing truth." He told Nicodemus that "doing truth" was really "work in God." What did he mean?

He meant that restitution is more than trying to be kind where we were unkind, or friendly where we were critical. We have to *do* truth! That may mean going to see someone, or making a telephone call, or writing a letter, or sending a check.

If we are in trouble — let's say at home — we try to patch things up with candy and flowers, or by baking a pie. But doing truth goes beyond that. It involves repenting and asking forgiveness.

Of course that's just our side. It is extremely important, but it is what God does that really makes the difference. All the management power belongs to him. He gives grace to the humble. He makes revival operational.

16

Competition

Many years ago Budd Schulberg wrote a best seller entitled *What Makes Sammy Run?* It is the story of an ambitious young movieman in Hollywood.

All my life I had been caught up in the same race with Sammy, on a different track, several laps behind.

As a university student I ran out of breath trying to create an image as a B.M.O.C. (big man on campus).

As a young newspaper reporter I chased after some of the "great ones" of my day: Cecil B. De Mille, Amelia Earhart, Babe Ruth, Harold Ickes, James A. Farley, Irving Berlin, Hendrik Van Loon, Peter B. Kyne.

As a minister I tied a kite string to my parish and ran harder than ever, trying to make it airborne. The congregation was not particularly responsive, because it didn't know where it was supposed to go. The more I worked, the slower things went, and one Sunday morning in the pulpit my throat gave out.

It took a good many years for me to realize that

Afterglow

Jesus didn't run at all. He was going by the sidereal clock of the universe. Time was his servant, not his master.

My model in those years was not Jesus so much as Alice in Wonderland, who found she had to run at full speed just to stay in the same place. Today it's called "spinning one's wheels."

I have discovered that the Holy Spirit is the only effective worker in spiritual affairs. Jesus said his yoke is easy and his burden is light. I don't run any more, neither do I spin wheels or operate off a discharging battery.

I have retired from the field and am letting the Spirit do it all. That means, of course, that I can no longer brag about what I'm doing for the Lord. But it never amounted to much anyway, and he knows it.

The point was brought home to me recently when I was invited to a certain city to preach in a church. I have relatives in that city, and they told me, "There's nothing in the paper about your coming."

A check of the church notices proved them right. Sensing an oversight, I drove past the church. The sign also said nothing. When I arrived at the church on Sunday morning, I was greeted and handed a bulletin. It also said nothing.

At the appointed time I preached the Gospel, and at the close the invitation was given. The space before the pulpit was crowded as people came seeking to be filled with the Holy Spirit and with love.

Driving home, I became aware of what had happened. The Spirit of God was at work and neither needed nor desired my little light to shine. The realization made my back hair crawl.

I knew then that my ego was anything but dead. So it was back to fundamentals: "I am crucified with Christ; . . . it is no longer I, but Christ who lives in me." "Be filled with the Spirit." "Let this mind be in you which was also in Christ Jesus."

A pastor friend of mine who had been revived was asked by a member of his church, "Reverend, why do you insist on talking all the time about being filled with the Spirit?"

My friend looked solemn. "Because," he said, "I leak."

17

The Pew and I

I don't know who invented the pew, but it wasn't Jesus. You won't find a pew in the whole New Testament.

There's nothing wrong with the pew (pew manufacturers, please note), apart from its shape. It seems to discourage Christians from praying for each other as they once did.

The early church, we have noted, believed Christians should pray specifically and personally for one another. James said, "Confess your faults one to another and pray one for another, that you may be healed."

Many Christians never get past the word "confess" in that verse, for it puts them off; but there is another verb in James 5:16: "pray." We are to lay hands on each other and pray for each other, not silently but vocally.

Jesus did it. Why is it we do not?

That brings us back to the pew. Have you ever tried kneeling in the space between two pews while laying your hand on someone's shoulder? It's enough to cause a slipped disc or even to cripple a person for life.

But you say, "We don't do that sort of thing in church." Why not? Didn't Jesus say, "My house shall be called a house of prayer"? And the psalmist said it before him. You reply, "Pews are for worship." But what is worship if not praise and prayer?

Of course we have churchly prayers, conducted by the people up front. Today's ecclesiastical architecture is admirably suited to pastoral prayer, silent prayer, musical prayer, antiphonal prayer, liturgical prayer, corporate prayer.

We can sit in our pews, listen to the minister, and pray silently for the President, the Vice President, the Congress, the Governor, the Mayor, the police, the Armed Forces, the missionaries, the sick, the sinners, the victims of famine and drought and fire and flood, those in prison, the pastor, the assistant pastor, the choir, the special meetings coming up, the young people on retreat at Camp Dripping Willows, and those who didn't quite make it to church.

But what about the person sitting next to us who came to church because he wanted desperately to get into touch with God? Who prays for him? Prayer might save his home, his sanity, even his life. And there he sits.

A few months ago I visited a small Midwestern town to help the church ladies of the region install their new district officers. After the meeting the new president asked to see me in the pastor's study. "My husband has left me," she said.

I expressed sympathy, but it was evident there was little that I, a visitor from another state, could do. Little — except pray.

"Do you have three or four friends here who would pray with us?" I asked. She did. We arranged to meet in ten minutes.

Soon a group of us gathered in the study. There

weren't enough chairs, but it didn't matter as we went to our knees. Hands were placed on the new leader. Intercession was offered. The president made a fresh commitment of her life. As we rose to our feet, one young woman wiped her eyes and said to no one in particular, *"Why won't they let us do this?"*

In that moment, for the first time, I became aware of something that has been keeping our churches from spiritual awakening. We simply have not been faithful to the New Testament requirement that we pray for each other.

To be sure, not everyone wants to be prayed for; many people would rather be left alone in their sin and misery. But what happens is that the least spiritually inclined have their way, and those hungry for fellowship with God and each other simply stay hungry.

Research indicates that a thousand years ago the pew was a kind of box used as a pulpit. It has been deteriorating ever since.

Once in an old book I came across a drawing of the upper room at Pentecost. It was quite graphic. Tongues of fire came down and sat on the heads of the disciples as they worshiped.

And where were the disciples? Sitting in pews.

When I saw it I groaned and thought, "No, Lord, whatever else happened at Pentecost, Your disciples were not sitting in pews."

Actually I have no idea whether they were sitting or kneeling or standing or prone. I understand the ancient Mediterranean culture did not possess an abundance of furniture. They probably had too many people for the indoor space and not enough lumber. Today many churches have too much lumber and not enough people.

Under the circumstances, when Christians want to pray for one another, they have to go to the social hall or to the church basement or into someone's home. Or they

Afterglow

temporize by saying, "I'll remember you in prayer."

That means presumably that one believer will go home, kneel at his bedside, and intercede for the other. Very good. But why not do it now, while they are together?

When people do pray for each other, hidden forces are released. Love bubbles to the surface. God opens fresh channels of communication. Jesus Christ becomes very real. The Holy Spirit works.

Pride is punctured. Hearts are humbled. Attitudes change. Homes are healed. The miracle of the Gospel occurs all over again as people become convinced that Christianity is a live option.

Amazing things happened when our Lord prayed for people. Amazing things still happen when we follow his example.

18

The Pit Stop

The apostle Paul felt it necessary to make a pit stop at church headquarters in Jerusalem, and I, with considerably less to go on, sensed a need to check with my Canadian teachers.

"Something's beginning to move," I told them. "Invitations are coming in that never came before. What shall I do?"

"Stay with Jesus," they said. "People want him, not you."

"Right. How much should I say about restitution?"

"That depends. How much restitution have you made?"

"I don't mean mine. Let's not talk about that. I mean when I'm talking to others."

"Not too much. The Holy Spirit works better by himself. It was Zacchaeus who talked about restitution, not Jesus."

Afterglow

"What if people speak in tongues at my meetings?"

"They're not your meetings, brother. Speak in love."

I asked for specific suggestions about the Afterglows. I was warned, "Don't turn it into a regular prayer meeting. You'll kill it."

"How do you avoid it?" I asked.

"Keep the people praying for each other, for those who are in the room. If they want to pray for an unsaved brother-in-law who works in a bar in Sheboygan, let them do it at the close, or invite them to the regular prayer meeting night. Or better, suggest that they ask God to give them more love for that person."

At first it seemed selfish. What good is the church, I wondered, if it can't open its heart to the need of the whole world? But the more I reflected, the more I realized the Canadians had something, and the church is in trouble right at that point.

The need of the world, desperate as it certainly is, can nevertheless become an excuse for failing to face up to our own difficulties. When that is the case, we come to church and play games. We cloak our problems in generalities. We wrap them in Elizabethan language and stuff them into the litany.

We do anything to avoid being candid and telling it the way it is. So the church becomes a showcase in which we appear with our best foot put carefully forward. No wonder the young people call us hypocrites!

And by ignoring the direct teaching of Scripture we miss out on the strength and courage and joy that come from being prayed for by brothers and sisters who are both loving and understanding. We also miss out on God's answers.

Just to make sure I was not being drawn into the trap of some ancient heresy, I went through the Gospels and the Book of Acts to see what kind of prayer the early disciples engaged in.

At Antioch, I found, the early Christians gathered around Paul and Barnabas, laid hands on them, and prayed for them. It didn't seem unusual.

At Miletus, when Paul stopped on his journey to Jerusalem, the church people came down from Ephesus, knelt on the beach, and prayed with him.

At Tyre the Christians came to the water's edge and did the same thing, and the wives and children joined in the prayers.

And in Galilee Jesus laid his hands on people and prayed for them.

What have we done to the church's prayer life? I wondered.

19

Mountains Into Molehills

Onlookers thought the early disciples who emerged from that Pentecost prayer meeting were drunk. After my brush with my northern friends I knew why. When you are filled with the Spirit you do feel a little drunk.

The cause is not alcoholic spirits, but the sudden departure of something out of your life. The desperate feeling, the trapped feeling, the bitter feeling, is subtracted from the body, you feel top-heavy and stagger a bit.

It's like trying to handle a ship after the cargo has been unloaded. It's like getting into your car in an airport parking lot, turning on the radio, and learning that the plane you just missed has been hijacked to Havana.

You know it's perfectly sappy to go around loving everyone, yet that's all you want to do. You listen to people putting down other people, and it sounds incongruous. You don't have anything against anybody.

To the Spirit-filled person, love says it all. The

apostle John put it, "If we love one another, God dwells in us and his love is completed in us. In this way we know that we dwell in him and he in us, because he has given us of his Spirit." Bless you, John.

I have learned there is no point in talking about strong churches and weak churches, big churches and little churches, warm churches and cold churches. Such categories are unrealistic and beside the point. There is only a loving church or an unloving church.

"I found," said a newly revived pastor, "that my church wasn't getting bigger, it was only getting fatter."

The Southern Baptists are supposed to have built their thousands of churches on zeal, but they didn't; they built them on love. The Pentecostals are supposed to run on special gifts of the Spirit, but they don't; they run on love. So do all the other churches and church organizations; and the way they love is the way they run.

When the church motors begin to sputter, don't blame the theology: Most of our churches honor the Bible as the Word of God. And don't blame the system of government: Most of our churches have adequate standing rules. Blame the lack of love!

The major reason for dissension and controversy in the body of Christ is simply that we don't love one another. It's such a simple thing, this love business, and we make it so complex. A child understands love. A pet understands love. But our pride tells us it's not enough to love; we have to prove our distinctiveness; we have to make clear to people that we "have something," that we are "successful."

So we develop a fresh vocabulary and talk about "community involvement," "social relevance," "penetration," "saturation," "ministry to the total man and the total woman." To which should be added the "evangelistic index."

This is all incidental to the work of the Holy Spirit. He supplies the fuel that runs the church. He pours in the love. He turns a congregation into a warm, friendly, loving group of people. And he never runs out of supply. There is no energy crisis with God.

Now, Christians don't always have to agree. The church has ample room for diversity — the New Testament says so. But when we stop loving, we go on tilt and everything begins to slide.

So what keeps us from loving each other? Memories, mostly. Our sour experiences. The build-up of resentment. We've been hurt once, and we don't want to be hurt again. We went for the loving bit in a big way, and it ended in disaster. Now we are cautious.

We will not wear our heart on our sleeve in church or anywhere else. We'll forgive (or say we do), but we won't forget. It's not that we carry a smoldering resentment (or do we?), not that we are actively hostile; we are just wary.

Only one word describes such a condition: bitterness. Life has made us bitter.

But in Winnipeg I was told that the Bible has another word for it: sin. Sounds strange, I know. We normally think the person who does the mistreating is the real sinner, not the one mistreated.

The Bible says both are sinners. One sins because he actively does wrong, the other because he holds a grudge. Grudges are the result of pride; and pride is man's original sin.

As I see it now, when we build a head of resentment against someone who has "pulled" something on us, it doesn't hurt him, but it tears us up, ruins our peace, and inflates our ego. We are proud that we are better, more righteous, more noble than he. That pride keeps us from forgiving, and it certainly keeps us from loving.

Afterglow

When we carry our resentment to church, the "koinonia" falls apart.

Let the minister preach up a storm; let the choir sing like angels. The commandment of Jesus has been broken and the church is in disrepair; the Holy Spirit has been grieved. Who can evangelize when love has slipped out?

Not until the breastworks of self-protection have been torn down and the mountains made back into molehills will the church once again become the church. And that is revival.

20

A Taxi to Inchon

I began to discover things in the Bible I had not noticed before, particularly in the New Testament. It was curious how this discovery came about. I was in Seoul, Korea, with the Billy Graham team in May 1973, covering a crusade for *Decision* magazine.

Members of the team were taking meetings in offices and factories and schools during the week, and I had been asked to help. On this particular afternoon, however, I had escorted our twenty-year-old Korean orphan daughter to the zoo. Winola and I had been sponsoring this young lady through "World Vision" for nine years, and I had just caught up with her.

When I returned to the Chosun Hotel, a platoon of Koreans and Americans charged me. "Where have you been?" they wanted to know.

I told them.

"Did you forget you were to speak to three thousand ROK army reserve troops at Inchon this afternoon?"

Afterglow

Unhappily my secretary and her datebook were on the other side of the planet in Minneapolis, Minnesota. I had blown it again.

My interpreter, Jonathan Lee, spoke. "We can still make it, but we must leave right now."

"But I — "

They shoved me through the revolving door and into a waiting taxi.

As we jolted through the streets of Seoul I tried to regroup my thoughts. Perhaps you could call it prayer. *What's going on, Lord? How could I have been so careless as to forget such an assignment? Was this your idea?* Fortunately my little New Testament was in my pocket. But what would I tell those soldiers? The Korean committee's instructions were clear: "They want you to preach the Gospel and give an invitation."

I thought about all those sermon outlines in my notebook at the hotel.

Jonathan opened his Korean Bible. "What Scripture will you be using?"

I had to say something. "What about the fourth chapter of Luke?"

"Luke. Very good. Is there a particular passage?"

"Try the fourteenth verse." I had just been reading that chapter in my devotions, and decided that what Jesus said in the synagogue at Nazareth about proclaiming the Good News would be a good note on which to begin. After that . . .

Jonathan began reading aloud: "And Jesus returned in the power of the Spirit into Galilee; and there went out a fame of him through all the region."

"Hold on," I said. "That's not the fourteenth verse."

"It is in Korean."

I dug out my Testament. "Something's wrong.

86

"Would you mind repeating it?"

Jonathan did. "And Jesus returned in the power of the Spirit into Galilee . . ."

Wheels began to turn in my mind. "Jesus in the power of the Spirit"? I hadn't paid any attention to that before.

Was it the same kind of thing that had happened to me? If it was —

21

The Wrong Text

While the taxi sped into the country, I continued to study Luke 4. I found in the opening verse that Jesus, "being full of the Holy Spirit, returned from Jordan."

There it was again. How could I have missed the significance of those words? What Jesus did, he did in the Spirit. When he went to the cross, according to his own statement, it was to release that same Spirit into the church.

Many things were falling into place. I could see that the ministry of Jesus in Galilee, Samaria, and Judea was a Spirit-filled one from beginning to end. But why had I never thought of it that way? Why had I never caught on to the way Luke emphasized it? And what about the rest of the New Testament?

We arrived at the ROK training camp and were rushed to headquarters, where the commanding general was awaiting us. There were introductions, tea was served, and we indulged in polite conversation. Then we were escorted onto a platform that faced a broad hillside. Here were the troops, thousands of them, seated in ranks, waiting patiently. *For what?* I wondered. *Lord, help me! No, don't help – just take over.*

After some musical numbers, Jonathan and I were introduced. I opened my New Testament to Luke 4:14: "Jesus returned in the power of the Spirit into Galilee."

I told the men that power was so important, Jesus couldn't minister without it. More than that, the Christian life could not be lived without it.

"Are you in the power of the Spirit?" I asked them. "Would you like that power? Would you like God to fill you with his Spirit? He will do it today."

Many Korean young men asked the Lord into their lives that afternoon. If there had been advance confusion about the text, it didn't matter: God knew what he was doing.

Samuel Chadwick once wrote that a day came in his life when his resources failed and he was "driven back upon God." He said that "this gave me a new Bible."

Since that day in Korea I have had a new Bible — so much so that I can absorb only a little of it at a time. The oil of the Spirit is, for me, high octane. I had no idea such power was loose in the pages of the New Testament.

I was beginning to sense what Peter and Paul and Stephen and Priscilla and Aquila were seeking to convey to their generation. They knew the inspiration of the Holy Spirit in a way we cannot comprehend or appropriate. But their footprints are still visible, and the trail can be traced.

22

Algebra Lesson

Billy Graham closed his gigantic Korean Crusade on a Sunday afternoon in June 1973. That same night I flew from Seoul across the Pacific to Hawaii and discovered upon arrival next morning at Honolulu's international airport that it was Sunday again.

By evening I was rested, and my island host said to me, "There are only three churches in town that are doing anything, and I'm taking you to one of them."

We drove to a modest church building and sat through a two-hour service, during which I discovered something I wished I had learned years before.

It is this: When a minister loves his congregation, really loves the people, and communicates that love so that they get the message, he can just about write his own ticket. I mean, the effective potential of that church has no limits.

Let me attempt to put it into simple algebraic terms. If A represents the minister, and B the congregation, and ∞ is the symbol of infinity, then $A + B = \infty$. Together the minister and the people can do anything.

Conversely, when a minister has an uncomfortable feeling that he is not getting across to his congregation, and the congregation picks up that kind of signal, the potential is minimal. In my kind of algebra the equation would read $A - B = Z$ (for zilch).

And there is a third equation. If a minister admits to a love for his congregation, *but not that much*, then he gets back a love, *but not that much*. The result is $\frac{1}{2}A + \frac{1}{2}B = 2C$ (for cold and clammy).

This Honolulu minister, to my observation, appreciated and cherished his people, and he made his point. He convinced me he was interested in them, not for what he could get out of them, but for themselves. He loved the people who were joining the church and the people who were leaving it.

His love was neither unctuous nor ostentatious nor professional; it was real and Christlike. He came from another part of the world, but he identified with Hawaii and entered into the experiences of the people. He preached a strong Gospel and kept his illustrations light, and they loved it.

The response was electric. So much goodwill was spread that when the offering was taken, the Bible camp fund was oversubscribed. The minister didn't ask for money; he simply said he knew the Lord would provide it.

It came to me that the real reason people join a church is not for the minister or the music or the convenient location. Surveys that draw this conclusion don't tell the whole truth.

People join churches because they find, or hope to find, love. They bring their God-shaped convictions with them, and thank God they do; but the reason they come into a fellowship is that someone has shown them love.

And here is the other half of my so-called understanding: When the people become aware that the minister loves them without put-on or hokum, they will give him back just about anything he wants, because he is giving them what *they* want.

To go back to the words of 1 John, "If we love one another, God dwells in us and his love is completed in us. In this way we know that we dwell in him and he in us, because he has given us of his Spirit."

If that is true, then the Holy Spirit is love. The power of the Spirit is the power of love. The breath of the Spirit is the breath of love. The flame of the Spirit is the flame of love. The unction of the Spirit is the unction of love. The baptism of the Spirit is the baptism of love. The filling of the Spirit is the filling of love.

As I flew from Honolulu to my Midwest home, one question remained to puzzle me: Why did it take so long for me to unravel all this?

23

Fire in the Pulpit

"If you want to warm up a church," Dwight L. Moody once said, "build a fire in the pulpit."

The Canadian revival as I observed it had a curious effect on the clergy.

Some said its greatest impact was on ministers; yet many pastors serenely ignored it. A British clergyman made a tour of western Canada's chief cities at the height of the revival and found "no trace of it."

Some opposed it on principle, saying revival was to be identified with fanaticism, mental illness, hypocrisy, racketeering, and so forth.

Some gave the appearance of welcoming it while hoping it would blow over and go away. When their people came to them, reporting personal renewal or other evidences of revival, they indicated no desire to be warmed, let alone scorched. They said in effect, "I believe in revival, but not in this revival."

When a revived Saskatoon minister visited a

seminary campus in the American Midwest, some of the students asked, "Why do we have to import the Holy Spirit?"

Some clergymen tried to capture the revival and absorb it into the program of their denomination, with results bordering on the hilarious. You just don't organize God! The One who structured the universe remains forever unstructured.

Some pastors were renewed. The revival knocked them off their pedestals — pedestals they didn't want and couldn't handle. As these preachers joined the rank and file on their knees in the church basement, God did an excellent thing in them.

Just as the sap makes an oak tree into a real oak tree, so the Holy Spirit makes a person into a real person. (I thank Ruth Graham for that remark.)

In the past three years I have met pastors whose ministries were transformed, and I have seen their congregations changed from pew-sitters into servants of the living God. Many pastors in prairie churches came alive spiritually and were given new assignments by the Holy Spirit. Two of them were called to be international evangelists.

But there is another side to the picture. During these months I have met many ministers who were discontented, heartbroken, and in despair. Some gazed longingly over the fence at greener pastures. Others have since taken to managing restaurants or selling insurance.

Is it possible for a spiritual leader beleaguered by church pressures, tempted by lust, frustrated by financial burdens, and harassed by domestic problems to be renewed in the midst of it all and turned into a powerful instrument of love?

The Bible says Yes. Jesus says Yes. The Holy Spirit says Yes.

24

The Body

At 100 Mile House, British Columbia, the elements had been prepared in a small church for Communion on Sunday morning. The minister was just back from a church convention in Vancouver.

Unknown to his members, the minister had received a touch of revival. That Sunday he told how God had plowed up his life, and when he finished, the congregation was weeping. Weeping not for its shepherd's sins but for its own.

The bread and wine went untouched that morning; the linen cloth stayed on the Communion table. A large number of church people came forward, not to the table, but to the altar. There was repentance and reconciliation and restitution.

The Communion service was held that evening, and what a service it was!

No finer sight is known to God or man than a revived minister of Christ. But his path to renewal is through thorns and thistles.

Afterglow

Many ministers ask for prayer in the Afterglows. Sometimes in a seminar on "The Spirit-filled Life," a minister will interrupt the speaker to request it.

"Do you mean you want prayer for yourself?"
"Yes."
"Now?"
"Yes."
"Here?"
"Yes."

We quickly place a chair so he can kneel with support, and some of the brothers and sisters gather around. When he stands up at the close of the prayers, someone else is there kneeling.

It is difficult to describe the intensity and earnestness of these servants of God as they seek to unload the spiritual baggage that has been holding back both them and their ministries.

One minister declared frankly that he was not interested in serving God. His efforts, he said, were devoted to impressing his congregation. "When I step into the pulpit, all I care about is, How will this sound to the crowd out there? I'm a phony," he concluded.

But I have yet to hear a minister ask others to pray with him and announce afterward that he has not been helped.

One pastor testified that he had expected nothing; that as he listened to people praying for him he was unmoved. Then he said he heard a voice he recognized as belonging to one of his church officers. He couldn't believe his ears. He had no idea the man loved him. "It broke me up," he said.

He wept. And he was filled with the Spirit.

In the spring of 1975 I was in Mississippi with Billy Graham, conducting a seminar on the Spirit-filled life for ministers and their wives.

A tall, young pastor remained afterward with a few others, all of whom wished to be prayed for. This young man said he had a problem of pride. Several of us knelt and prayed, asking God to humble him. A week later he telephoned me in Minnesota in great excitement: God was beginning to move in his congregation. At the evening service the people had met in small groups and had prayed for each other. "For the first time," he said, "I have seen people leaving our church in tears."

Sometimes it is not the minister who needs to be defrosted but the congregation. Sometimes it's both.

People are used to sitting under a preacher week after week and hearing him lead in prayer during the service. Then one day they find him on his knees alongside them, praying for them. It does something to them. They don't forget.

In the same way, the pastor hears people tell him they are praying for him. Unfortunately they seldom do it when he is around to hear it. They leave him on a lofty height; and whoever heard of a lofty height needing to be filled with love and to have its sagging spirit lifted?

The New Testament says, "Pray one for another." In the body!

25

The Gal in the Parsonage

Principal Robert Rainy, one of the great Scottish ministers of the last century, was stopped one day on Edinburgh's Princes Street by a fellow clergyman who wanted to know how Mr. Rainy could look so cheerful. Didn't he know that the leaders of the church were at his throat and that his career was in jeopardy?

Said Rainy by way of reply, "I'm happy at home."

My experience as husband of a minister's wife is atypical, since my wife had to lead her balky horse from the fringes into the Christian faith. Yet I can confirm one conclusion of the Canadian revival: The minister's wife is the key to much of what happens in a church.

The Afterglows have revealed that if love is to blossom in the church, it has to bud in the parsonage. Only in the last three years have I understood God's order of priorities.

Show me a minister's wife with a lot of love, and I'll show you a church. Show me a minister's wife with a hang-up, and I'll show you a hang-up.

Let's be fair about this: A lot of the problems of the minister's wife are not of her own making. It would be a gross injustice to blame her for the church's condition. But when she is having a difficult time, many people become involved.

A recent American study reported that ministers' wives suffer the highest casualty rate of any vocational group in our time.

So the sociologists have isolated the trouble area. Their pathology is right on. What about the therapy?

At an Afterglow one minister's wife said, "I didn't want to move to this church. My children were happy where they were. I couldn't see why God would shove us around like this. I wanted nothing to do with the new congregation."

After she had asked people for prayer and had asked God to fill her with the Holy Spirit, she told her own congregation how she felt. The church members identified with her honesty, sympathized, and — as she wept and told of her new love for them — took her to their hearts. Now she wouldn't be anywhere else.

Yes, the minister programs the church. Yes, he sets the church's theological tone and life-style after a few years. No one would think of denying his importance.

But back of Aquila is Priscilla.

Back of Martin Luther is Katie von Bora.

Back of Jonathan Edwards is Sarah Pierrepont.

Back of David Livingstone is Mary Moffat.

Back of Billy Graham is Ruth Bell.

A minister's wife can look at the church in different ways. She can see it as The Drain. It siphons off her man's time and energy until he has none left for her. This condition creates a familiar and predictable anticlerical attitude; she wishes he would go back to his job in the complaint department of the zipper factory.

She can see it as The Duty. It is a full-time, non-salaried job which she discharges from a sense of obligation. She can be found at all hours, teaching, calling, arranging programs, telephoning, driving people here and there, playing the piano, burning out her motor.

Or she can see the church as Jesus saw it — as a House of Prayer.

When the church is a Drain, God becomes an object of hostility and is eventually despised. When the church is a Duty, he becomes a tyrant and is eventually hated. When the church is a House of Prayer, God becomes the one who hears and answers prayers.

If I read my New Testament correctly, it teaches that God does not lay on us more than we can bear. He is our loving Father. In his sight the minister's wife is neither a minister nor a wife, but a human being and his child.

She is someone beloved and cherished, someone valued not for what she does, but for who she is. Christ went to the cross, not to give her enough work for three people, but to take away her sin and fill her with his Spirit.

I am enormously impressed by the personal qualities of the ministers' wives I have been privileged to meet. They are among society's choicest — and most sensitive — servants. No human measuring stick can gauge the help they give to their husbands.

In church after church the congregation rises up and calls this woman blessed. How tragic, then, that she should so often crack up!

I don't have the answer to her problem. But I have discovered that when a minister's wife has received a supernatural touch of the love of God, and has conveyed that love to the people around her, they have been quick to respond.

Does she pray? They will pray with her.
Does she study the Word? They will sit at her feet.

Afterglow

Does she love Jesus? They will come into a new love for him.

Does she weep for the needs of others? They will do more than weep, they will go into action.

Is she contented with her role? They are a happy people.

26

"I Love You, Dick"

By now you know the grim truth: This book contains little original thinking. I met some people who were revived, and quite unexpectedly I was revived. What they taught is what you get.

One lesson I have learned is that we Christians are not successfully evangelizing our families because we come across with a weak performance. By the time we get around to making our pitch, no one wants to buy. The non-Christians in our families avoid Christian contacts not because of Jesus, but because of us. There may be exceptions to that statement, but I'll stand on it.

Let's create an imaginary scene. Mrs. Richard Loner returns from attending her church's Sunday evening service and is greeted by her husband, who is watching television. He turns down the volume politely and we pick up the dialogue.

Hi. How was the meeting?

Afterglow

Just wonderful, Dick. I'm in a glow. There must have been thirty young people there, and they sang beautifully.

That's nice. Who preached?

The pastor. I always get so much out of his teaching. My Bible is full of notes. Oh, and Jim Turner was there and asked after you.

Well, you missed a good program. Oh, uh, I think Cindy is getting a sty in her eye. I gave her something to wash it out.

I'll go up and take a look. Dick?

Huh?

Am I going to have to go to church by myself for the rest of my life?

I wouldn't say so. You can always stay home.

That's not what I mean and you know it. Why don't you go with me?

Oh, I dunno.

You ought to believe in Christ.

Maybe I do.

How can you? I never see you reading the Bible.

Well, I –

What have you got against the church?

Nothing. I just never thought there was anything there for me.

Don't you believe in hell?

Look, sweetheart, are you going to look after that kid or not?

Yes, I will. But how do you think I feel, always having to go to church by myself?

I dunno. How do you feel?

Will you come next Sunday?

Oh –

The reader is invited to fill out the last line by himself.

Now, let's assume that something has happened to Mrs. Loner. She has read a passage of Scripture or has heard a message or has prayed with a fellow Christian, and the Holy Spirit has shown her her own need.

Remember what was said in an earlier chapter: "You can't change anybody, but God can change you."

Let's see what happens when she comes home on Sunday evening.

Hi. How was the meeting?
Fine. And how are you? I missed you.
I missed you too. Who preached?
The pastor. He talked about love. He said to tell you I love you, so here's a kiss, and I do love you. Do you believe that?
Say it again.
Would you like me to fix you a little snack?
That might be nice. Cindy has a sty, I think. I gave her something to wash it out.
I'll look after her. But first I'm taking care of you.
Why the sudden special treatment?
I just feel loving. You're a pretty nice guy.
I wasn't aware of it.
I think you are. And you're my dear husband, and I'm your obedient wife.
Well, blow the man down.
Want some coffee?
Why not! Guess I've been kind of ornery lately. Things on my mind . . . .Tell me, did they put the fear of hell into you over at that church? Is that what's got into you?
I don't love you just because the Bible tells me to. I love you because you're my husband. . . . Jim Turner spoke to me.
What about?

Afterglow

He says they're getting up a tournament and wants to know if you'll play.
Really? When?

Jesus came to bring love to the human race. When we convey that love and make it stick, the Holy Spirit moves in and softens the beachhead. Evangelism becomes a procedural rather than a substantive issue.

27

The Accuser

Kneeling and praying alongside Christian brothers and sisters, I have learned something about the inroads Satan has made in their spiritual lives.

Not that the Afterglows have produced a rash of confessing! In three years I have heard nothing that goes beyond the canons of modesty and good taste. The Holy Spirit has monitored the sessions in ways no human being could have.

Actually the people sitting in the circle are in prayer and hear little of what is spoken in the center. All they know is that someone is doing business with God.

As I look back to the years before 1971, I realize that my approach to other people's problems was conditioned by my own situation. I thought I was a freak; surely other born-again Christians didn't let themselves get into a box as I had done.

Today I know that other people who love Jesus Christ — thousands of them — are in serious predicaments just as I was. When I try to explain this state of affairs, the only answer I can find is that Satan is making a frontal assault on the church.

Scripture gives Satan many names. He is called the adversary, the devil, the enemy, the father of lies, the angel of the bottomless pit, the murderer, the old serpent, the power of darkness, the prince of this world, the prince of devils, the prince of the power of the air, the ruler of darkness, the tempter, the wicked one, the great red dragon, and so on.

But there is one title given him that relates to us where we live. In Revelation 12:10 he is described as "the accuser of our brothers," the one who "accuses them before God day and night."

That title fits. I have prayed with Christians of many different persuasions who were squirming under a secret load of guilt. Their consciences kept reminding them of their unworthiness, and they seemed to believe that God would have it no other way.

As a young pastor I tried to comfort a man who had lost a son in the bombing of Pearl Harbor. The father wept as he told me, "It was for my sins that God took my boy from me."

It is not for me to pass judgment on that situation. What I do say is that Christians need to "discern the spirits" and to spot the accuser when he attacks.

Our consciences can lead us to genuine contrition over things we have done and can draw on all the resources of God to set our feet on the right path. But conscience can also be taken over by Satan and used to distort a situation out of all proportion to the truth.

In some mysterious way Pentecost has made a difference here. Jesus sent the Holy Spirit into the church to thwart the accuser and nail his lies.

So a Christian who finds himself involved in a situation with gray areas in it does not need to keep going back over the circumstances and blaming himself. If he has acknowledged his fault, asked forgiveness of God and man, done the right thing in making restitution as far as he can, he need lose no sleep about it. God is not the persecutor of our souls.

Satan's idea is to keep us day and night weeping for our sins, grieving over our failures, lamenting our mistakes. He wants us to wallow in inner recrimination, anguish of heart, self-blaming, and self-reproach.

He knows how sensitive we are, and he exploits our moral sense. We will be confronted with a matter, and after prayer we will lay it upon the altar of the Lord and leave it. But Satan says to us, "You can't do that. What about this person or that person?"

So we try to satisfy him at one point, and as soon as we do he begins nagging us at another. As long as he can keep us spiritually off balance and powerless at all times, Satan is content. Millions of hours of effective Christian service are lost to God because we insist on listening to another voice.

When a Christian is filled with the Holy Spirit, it is not hard for him to recognize the accuser when he attacks. The Christian can sort out the matter because he is getting the right kind of "input."

When we attune our ears to the voice of the Spirit of God, we are not disappointed. He may speak to us through God's Word, or in some other manner of his choosing, but the result is the same. When we obey him, he gives us instant peace.

That's how we know.

28

The Golden Pitcher

Corrie ten Boom told the story at the Lausanne Congress in 1974.

After World War II, while she was speaking to a German audience, she spotted a woman who had mistreated her and her sister, Betsie, at Ravensbrück concentration camp during the war. The woman had worked for the Gestapo as a nurse. Betsie had died as a result of the mistreatment.

A wave of hatred came over Corrie as she recognized the woman, and she realized she had not forgiven her. Corrie remembered what Jesus had said about forgiving others if we are to receive his forgiveness.

Yet there she was, filled with hate, talking away to the Germans about Christian love.

At that point, as Corrie tells it, she "cashed the check of Romans 5:5." After the meeting she sought out the woman and found her to be quite a frightened person. Corrie made friends with her and eventually was able to lead her into a personal relationship with Jesus Christ.

As I sat listening to the story I wondered, What is Romans 5:5? Opening my New Testament, I read, "The love of God is poured out in our hearts by the Holy Spirit which is given to us."

The words jumped out at me. Lord, I thought, give me that again. It was what I had been searching for: a New Testament description of the work of the Holy Spirit as love.

I felt like standing on my chair and announcing the discovery to the entire International Congress on World Evangelization. Instead I went back to the passage, turning the words around so they read, "The Holy Spirit, which is given to us, pours out the love of God into our hearts."

Why? For what reason does the Holy Spirit do this?

So we can love, obviously.

I began thinking about that expression *poured out*. It seemed to me that my life could be described as a glass. (In the old days it would probably have been called a "vessel.") I saw that God has a golden pitcher, and he proposes to fill that glass with living water. He wants to fill it and keep on filling it until it overflows. He wants it to splash into other glasses around, and that's witnessing.

The overflow of a Spirit-filled life is the kind of witnessing that built the early church. And it's still the only kind that gets through to the unbeliever. I believe that without the Holy Spirit, witnessing is harder than door-to-door vending. I've tried both.

When the water is spilling over the brim, talking about Jesus becomes easy. The Lord prepares everything; he sets up the appointments, arranges the interviews, draws the interest, brings off the result.

The trouble was, God couldn't fill my glass.

There was no problem at the Source; the artesian

wells of Infinity are inexhaustible. The problem was with me. There was already water in my glass, and it was polluted. Sediment lay on the bottom. It had to be tipped upside down and emptied.

Jesus said in John 7:38,39 that living water would flow from those who believed in him. He was speaking about the Holy Spirit.

But God will not mix pure water with impure. He will not pour from his golden pitcher until our glass has been drained. He will not send his love into a heart that is already in love with itself, or his power into a life operating under human power.

Now I saw more clearly what Paul meant by saying, "I am crucified with Christ."

Not until after his crucifixion did our Lord send the Holy Spirit into the church. That's why he went to the cross. Not just to take away our guilt and shame, but to send power by his Spirit. Power to live and power to love.

What about us? Well, the same thing has to happen. We must go to the cross — not only to kneel in reverence, not only to bow in commitment, not only to pick up our cross and carry it, but to be crucified.

Self-crucifixion means that Christ will send his power into us as individual selves by the same Spirit. But first, as Richard Bennett says, the Christian has to attend his own funeral — willingly.

Why wasn't I filled with the Spirit long ago? I don't know. When will God revive the church? I don't know that either.

But this I do know: The water will not flow until the glass has been tipped upside down and emptied.

29

Articulating the Faith

Early in the seventies I listed what I thought were ten major characteristics of the Holy Spirit as I found them in the Bible. Today I would put love ahead of all of them.

At a recent conference on evangelism in St. Andrews, Scotland, I heard a clergyman say, "We must train our laymen to articulate the faith so they can go out and win others to Christ."

It reminded me of a time when I was pastoring a church, and received a notice from headquarters instructing me to train my laymen in evangelism. I called a meeting of the church leaders, and we arranged a fall program. Once a week a group of us met at night and went through the manual of instructions. Then we went out knocking on doors.

It didn't work.

The next fall another package of material arrived from headquarters. It contained a fresh manual of instructions. That didn't work either.

Afterglow

So it went. We didn't grow much, but I'll tell you, we had the most highly trained laymen in the history of evangelism. For being nonproducers, we certainly knew our stuff.

I'm blaming no one but myself. I should have known that before laymen can articulate the faith, something must happen to the laymen.

But first something had to happen to me.

Before we can become witnesses to Christ, we need to be filled with God's love. We need to feel the compassion Jesus had for the lost multitudes. We need to give ourselves over to the grace and mercy of God so that God can do what he wants through us.

And how do you work that?

You don't. You do nothing except "cash the check." Paul's key to the spreading of the Gospel was, "Be filled with the Spirit."

Juan Carlos Ortiz of Buenos Aires said at the Lausanne Congress, "Love is the key to world evangelization." He very nearly said it all.

Some Christians will evangelize from a sense of duty, but they will catch few salmon. They will try to win souls because they don't wish to let their pastor down (or to have him think they are letting him down), but they will dig up few clams.

A few decades ago I owned a little, yellow Model A Ford roadster, the joy of my life. I neglected to put oil in it, and one day a connecting rod ripped through the block. End of automobile.

Without the oil of the Spirit, the church soon generates friction. It may look cute with its lawn and patio, but give it time and it will end up like my Model A Ford.

Then it's everyone out and push. Heave — heave — heave. That's no way to operate a vehicle — or a church.

David Wilkerson said to me, "The baptism of the

Holy Spirit is a baptism of love that God poured out on the whole church at Pentecost."

To make that baptism a fact in the local church, our hearts need to say to the Lord, "Thy face, Lord, will I seek." We have to look, seek, hunger, thirst, until we are willing to face up to what we really are.

The moment we begin to humble ourselves we have moved onto the launching pad.

God does the rest. Love becomes the catalyst, and church growth begins to appear. It can't help appearing. People don't get turned on to Jesus and then keep him to themselves. They have to share him.

Articulate? You can't shut 'em up!

30

God's Will

I guess I have read a score of books about the will of God: how to discern it, recognize it, know it, get into the center of it, obey it, and so on.

If I recall correctly, we discover the will of God in four tried and tested ways: first, through prayer; second, through the reading of God's Word; third, through counsel with other Christians (including the guidance of parents); and fourth, through the events and circumstances in which we find ourselves (including notices from the government).

But it still stacks up as a mystery. Especially when the person we have trusted lets us down. Or a car accident befalls us on the way to church.

In the poem by Stephen Vincent Benét, "John Brown's Body," Abraham Lincoln complains about the difficulty of discovering God's will. To paraphrase Benét, Lincoln says one would think that instead of sending delegations of clergy to the White House to inform him of his will, God might have made his will known directly, the more so since he, Lincoln, earnestly desired to know God's will.

Many kings and presidents have yearned to discover God's will.

Being filled with the Spirit has not made me wiser than they; in fact it is a disappointment to discover that my intelligence has not been affected by revival. (I was hoping for a fringe benefit.)

But I have learned something I didn't know about the will of God. It is his will that we should love.

Do you want to know God's will for your life? It's love. Start there.

The way to get a positive answer to prayer is to pray in God's will. How do we do that? We ask God for the thing he wants to give us. And that's love. When we love, we are squarely in the center of God's will.

Let's say we have a choice to make, and we are praying for God to reveal his will in the matter. We don't have to pray, "Lord, I want what you want." We already know what he wants: He wants us to start loving.

"Love your enemies," said Jesus. "Bless them that curse you, do good to them that hate you, and pray for them that despitefully use you and persecute you."

Love your relatives, especially those who don't agree with your theological position.

"When we love one another, God dwells in us, and his love is completed in us."

I remember how God used Mother Wells to heal my split theological personality when I was living in her home and attending a seminary whose views clashed with hers.

Each morning I would push my bicycle up the hill to absorb the urbane opinions of such New Testament scholars as Shirley Jackson Case, Morton Scott Enslin, and Henry J. Cadbury. Then at night I would coast home to a heavy dosage of Harry A. Ironside, Donald Grey Barn-house, and Wilbur M. Smith, all of them evangelical fire-brands. Mother had their tracts!

I felt as if I were holding an ice cube and a hot potato in my mouth at the same time. Month after month it went on, and instead of getting better it grew worse.

Then one day after a routine run-through of Daniel's ten horns and seventy weeks, Mother said to me, "Sherwood, I don't wish you to think I'm trying to prove you wrong, or that I have anything against anyone. I tell you these things because I love you."

That tore it. With the "consensus of scholarly opinion" at my command, I could have put down every theological and historical argument she raised before she even brought it up.

But I couldn't withstand her love. It made a believer of me.

Now I am prepared to take on the "scholarly consensus" myself with some heavy back-up artillery, but it develops that there really isn't any such thing. The nineteenth-century critical monolith is crumbling, while every dilettante in hermeneutics proposes what is right in his own eyes.

I knew Mother had something I didn't have, but a fierce pride prevented my admitting it. When she turned on the love, Jericho's walls came down.

God goes where love is. That's how he works. He has said so, and he never lies. He does what he says he will do. Every time.

31

A New Bible

Many years ago I became convinced the Bible is fully inspired. I knew this inspiration to be the work of God the Holy Spirit. I also knew that the Holy Spirit is the Third Person of the Trinity and Lord of the church. As I have said, I had a theological appreciation of him, but much of my knowledge in this area could be classified as vague and blurry.

My condition was not far different from the Mandarin convert of pre-Maoist China who, it is said, complained to his missionary teacher, "Honorable Father, understand. Honorable Son, understand. Honorable Bird, no understand."

In the last three years I have been given an entirely new appreciation of Scripture. Since that day in Korea when I discovered that Jesus came into Galilee in the power of the Spirit, I have been looking at God's Word through a different set of lenses. Time after time I have been jolted to see how the New Testament speaks of the

Afterglow

Holy Spirit. Let me cite a few examples:

In Ephesians 5:18 Paul writes, "Be not drunk with wine, wherein is excess; but be filled with the Spirit."

Why did the apostle contrast the filling of the Spirit with inebriation? Because there are instructive similarities and dissimilarities. Liquor promises a lot and puts on quite a front, but its windup is notoriously better than its delivery. Liquor is a waste (which is the real meaning of the Greek word for "excess"). The end of liquor is the chemical dependency ward.

But everything that liquor promises and fails to produce, the Spirit makes available. The end of the Spirit is Christ.

In Romans 8:5,9 Paul writes, "Those who live according to the flesh set their minds on the things of the flesh, but those who live according to the Spirit set their minds on the things of the Spirit. . . . But you are not in the flesh, you are in the Spirit, if in fact the Spirit of God dwells in you" (RSV).

Even now I can hear the droning voice of my New Testament professor of thirty years ago: "In this polarization of flesh and spirit we see characteristic evidence of Hellenistic influence on Paul's thinking . . ."

I read such passages these days from an entirely new perspective. When Paul uses the word Spirit, I sense he is speaking of a friend of mine; in other words, I know whom he is talking about. When Paul says the Spirit is life, I agree. When he says the people of God are led by the Spirit of God, I can identify with him. When he says the Spirit sets us free, I jot some exclamation points in the margin!!!

The Gospel of John has been the chief enlightener as I have sought to grasp afresh the supernatural aspect of Calvary. Chapters 14 - 16 have made it clear that back of Jesus' vicarious sacrifice was his desire to impart to us the Holy Spirit. This desire became a reality at Pentecost.

Just as his blood washed away our past guilt, so his Spirit gives us present power to live for Christ.

Perhaps the most significant description of the work of the Spirit is contained in John 16:13,14: "He shall not speak of himself; but . . . he shall glorify me."

So the works of the Spirit are to give us gifts and to cause us to bear spiritual fruit and to fill us with love for each other; but the mission of the Spirit is simply to glorify Jesus.

What about secret prayer and formal worship and evangelism and social concern and the other things the Bible talks about? I believe in all of them and work at all of them. I don't know any Christian worth his salt who doesn't.

But we must face the fact that the church is suffering from its own energy crisis. The oil shortage facing Western civilization is nothing to the oil shortage facing the church. And the oil of the Spirit is not found by sinking a shaft.

Without the Holy Spirit we cease to be missionaries and become mission fields. Jesus warned us not to expect the blind to lead the blind.

It is tragic to think that if the Holy Spirit were to leave some of our churches, he would not even be missed.

It is the Spirit who interprets to us the mysteries of the Bible. He explains the Resurrection; he explains the miracles; he explains the living and indwelling Christ; and he prepares us for the return of Christ.

Not only does he tell us how to live the Christian life, but he lives it through us. We can't make it without him.

32

Priorities

The Canadian revival — in its first phase — is over. Many people didn't know it had begun. As far as I am aware, not a single interdenominational church gathering has taken notice of it.

Ralph and Lou Sutera, the American evangelists whom God used so remarkably in Saskatoon in 1971 and elsewhere since, are continuing to hold meetings in the power of the Spirit.

From a modest office in Regina, Saskatchewan, the Canadian Revival Fellowship (organized in 1972) reports an increasing number of inquiries from all over the world, asking for news of revival activity. Teams, books, tapes, and tracts are going out in a steady stream. Great blessings are reported in letters from churches and individuals.

But the Saskatoon explosion that made brief newspaper headlines in October and November 1971 is finished. The original impetus that was used of the Spirit of God to revive scores of congregations in British Columbia, Alberta, Saskatchewan, and Manitoba is no longer present. That, too, is part of God's sovereign plan.

Other great spiritual developments are taking the world's center stage — developments more significant in human eyes and possibly in God's economy. Problems of world hunger, of energy shortages, of increasing religious and racial hostility, are dominating the seventies.

Meanwhile, as religious and psychological fads come and go and the options open to seekers turn out to be dead ends, the opportunities for evangelical Christians to spread the Gospel throughout the Western world are proving unparalleled.

In Latin America, in Africa south of the Sahel, and in some parts of Asia, the churches are growing at an unprecedented pace. Persecution is growing, too, but through it all the name of Jesus is being magnified.

Perhaps God is about to visit the human race with a revival, the nature of which is presently inconceivable to us. It may well be the prelude to the climax of history as recorded in Matthew: "This gospel of the kingdom shall be preached in all the world for a witness unto all nations; and then shall the end come."

In the face of all these tremendous movements, the affair in western Canada seems small indeed. It just happened to be a touch of love that reached across the border and found me in Minnesota.

It met my need and forced me to reorder my priorities. In a way it was exasperating to spend years trying to change other people and then discover that what God wanted to change was me. The impact I had hoped to leave on my world was nothing to the impact the Holy Spirit made on me. He sent me back to Square One.

As Vance Havner would say, I had to cut out all the theological grand opera and go back to practicing the scales.

Instead of talking and writing about the cross, I was nailed to it. Instead of taking up the problems of humanity and trying to unravel them, I faced up to my own. Instead of urging others to be unselfish, I was emptied of self. And instead of going through life spiritually dehydrated, I fell into a vat full of love.

One result has been a different kind of home. In a way Winola hasn't changed; she warned me that she wouldn't back in 1940 when we were courting on the S.S. *Alaska*. But of course, in other ways she has changed greatly, and I have changed too. And things are better. There's prayer. There's Bible study. And there's about 1,000 percent more love.

I have learned that (allowing for Satan's tricks and other exceptions) if a Christian doesn't make it at home he doesn't make it.

Time was when we couldn't drive to church without an argument springing out of nothing. That has changed. We leave certain things alone and enjoy each other's company. What a delightful person God has given me for a partner!

Best of all for me, the fundamental discontent with life has been replaced by an inner peace and happiness, and a sense of being used.

To the men and women whom God revived in Canada go my perpetual thanks. The names of those I know, and some whom I have never met, will always carry a special meaning in my heart. So will the names of the friends who have gone to distant places with me and have prayed, hour after hour, in the Afterglows.

I have tried to tell the story of the past three and a half years without really comprehending what has happened. Call it revival, renewal, a fresh touch, an anointing, times of refreshing, or what you will. I needed it.

But this has not been just my story. It belongs to the churches of Canada and America and the world. It is a

Afterglow

story of congregations that couldn't get to Jesus because they seemed to be stuck in their pews. A story of Christian brothers and sisters closing ranks; of clergymen coming off their eminence; of people walking in a brand-new world.

It is a beautiful thing to learn that the Holy Spirit is love. As Barb Egle, a young Mennonite girl, said during an Afterglow in an Illinois country church, it's like having an exciting new Person in your life.